The Czech Republic -

The Most Haunted Country in the World?

By

G. Michael Vasey

Text and photographs copyright 2016: G. Michael Vasey
ISBN: 978-0-9961972-3-6

Contents

Introduction

The Czech Republic is a beautiful, landlocked country at the heart of Europe. This central European country has a pagan Slavic past that has survived and indeed, even been adopted in some ways, by Christianity. From whipping girls with special sticks at Easter to visits from the Devil, an Angel, and St. Nicholas on St. Nicholas' day, there are reminders of the country's past paganism at every turn during the course of a year. It is a country where every town and city has its own ghost stories, legends, and myths. It is a country where innumerable castles dot the landscape and are separated by haunted and magical forests. Each castle has its hidden treasures, specters, and wraiths. The Czech Republic may just be the most haunted country on the planet!

Central and eastern Europe was until recently more or less inaccessible to most westerners. Hidden behind the 'iron curtain' for many years, this part of Europe is cloaked in a veil of mysteriousness, gothic horror, and strange magical tales like that of Count Dracula or the Prague Golem. Romania and Czechoslovakia are both names that evoke a sense of the supernatural because of their strange and often terrifying, myths and legends. The lack of access to these countries during communism simply accentuated this reputation. These days, millions of tourists pour into Prague, Bratislava, Budapest, and other beautiful yet mysterious cities, to explore their history, architecture, and culture. Hidden just beneath the surface however, there is a murky undercurrent of occult, alchemy, myth, legend, and the supernatural that pervades the atmosphere of such places.

Living in the Czech Republic (Czechoslovakia split in two after the fall of communism), I have had more than a decade to explore and soak up this mysterious and often scary undercurrent personally. In this book, I will introduce you to some strange and even terrifying places; the supernatural history that is at the heart of the Slavic culture and awe you with ghost and undead stories that in all likelihood, you have never heard before. Join me now as we explore together the Haunted Czech Republic.

The Origins of a Nation

Much can be discerned about a place and its people based on its origins and the beginnings of the Czech Republic are shrouded in ancient pagan myth and legend. Many of today's rural Czechs in particular still engage in strange pagan traditions that have long since lost their true meaning such as beating young women at Easter with special wooden sticks and having a visit from the Devil just before Christmas!

The original Czechs arrived some 1500 years ago, probably from the Black Sea and Carpathian mountains, bringing their Slavic language and pagan religions with them. Their cultural essence is what has shaped the nation ever since.

Říp and Čech

Czech legend says that a man named Čech (pronounced 'Chek') founded the Czech Republic. He had murdered someone in his homeland and was forced into exile as punishment. He set out to find another place to live along with his tribe with either two or three brothers (the other two were Lech and Mech – pronounced 'Lek' and 'Mek') depending on the version of the story that you read. The three or sometimes two brothers finally arrived at a mountain just north of Prague called Říp – an extinct volcano with a rather unique shape that rises from flat plains very abruptly. Čech climbed the mountain and looked around him. He saw the beautiful land that became their homeland called Čechy (pronounced 'Chekee'). He reputedly told his people at the top of the mountain,

"Oh, comrades, you've endured hardships along with me, when we wandered in impassable woods; finally we arrived at our homeland. This is the best country, predestined for you. Here you won't miss anything, but you'll take pleasure in permanent safety. Now that this sweet and beautiful land is in your hands, think up a suitable name."

Figure 1: A View of Říp

His brothers, Lech and Mech, continued onwards, so the legends say, founding Poland and Russia, where they too, finally settled. This founding myth of the Czech Republic is thought by many academics to have been inspired by the biblical founding of Israel as Čech is also said to have talked about the land that he saw from Říp as the land of '*milk and honey*'.

The Slavs replaced the Celts and the Germans who had inhabited the region previously. They soon developed a social structure and had a mythical forefather who was named Krok. Krok was said to be both wise and very just and he was made Duke or Judge of the Czech people because of this wisdom. He and his wife had three daughters. Their eldest daughter, Kazi, is said to have known every plant and was a healer, a pythoness and Fate; their second daughter, Teta, taught the Bohemians how to worship their deities and gods; while he youngest daughter, Libuše, was a prophetess. Libuše is said to have been so chaste and kindly that the Bohemians elected her as Judge after her father's death. You may note that in this legend Krok's three daughters are endowed with certain magical powers and in some ways, they mirror the three Fates of Greek mythology.

Přemysl and Libuše

Libuše's rule was the subject of some discontent as she was a woman and many Czechs felt that a man was required to lead the nation. She was told to marry to rectify this issue. In response, she told her people that she had had a vision in which she saw a farmer with one broken sandal ploughing in a field (or in other versions of the same legend, eating from an iron table). She told the people to let her white

Figure 2: Divoka Šárka in Prague

horse go free, as this horse would lead them to this man that she had seen in her vision. The horse led everyone to the village of Stadice and there they found a man named Přemysl exactly as she had foretold. Přemysl was taken back to the palace where Libuše married him, and Přemysl the Ploughman, became the ruler of the Czechs.

Přemysl naturally began to favor the men of the land, causing one of Libuše's handmaidens to rebel against male rule. In the so-called "Maidens war", women murdered men and made war against them in what may have been the very first battle of the sexes. Přemysl eventually won and soon put an end to this war. However, according to the legend, the war continued for some time until a young maiden named Šárka set up a trap for Ctirad, the greatest fighter from the opposing all-male army. Using her feminine charms, Šárka positioned herself so the men would find her staked to a tree. She told them that she had been captured by a band of the warring maidens and then used her beauty to persuade Ctirad to set her free. Once free, she gave Ctirad and his men some honeyed wine, which the warriors of course drank until they passed out drunk. Then, the rest of the maidens jumped out and killed all the men, except Ctirad, who was taken as their prisoner. The beautiful area in Prague known as Divoka Šárka is where this was supposed to have taken place and why the location apparently got its name.

It was also Libuše who foresaw in another of her miraculous visions, that there would one day be a major city 'reaching to the skies' on the other side of the Vltava River from where they had built their castle at Vyšehrad; she named it Praha (Prague).

Seven is an occult number that occurs over and over again in myth, legend, and even the Bible; such as the seven days, seven planets, seven tones or notes, and much more. Přemysl and Libuše eventually gave birth to the first generation of the legendary *seven* generations of Dukes or Princes who ruled Čechy. Their names have been argued by scholars to refer to the names of the Gods whose names are used to construct the names of the days of the week. For example, Thursday or Thor's Day, is likened to the name Křesomysl, the sixth Duke or Prince, whose name may be based on the Czech word *křesat,* which can mean to strike or be striking.

Hormír and his Talking Horse

Křesomysl was also the richest of the seven Dukes because he had discovered silver in the Czech lands and he began to mine it. In fact, he even encouraged his people to abandon farming to become silver miners instead. One farmer, a man named Horymír, who lived in the village of Neumětely, and owned a white horse of great intelligence called Šemík, disagreed. He was unhappy with Křesomysl's rule and his focus on silver mining because he believed that encouraging people to become miners rather than farmers would one day result in widespread famine.

His dispute with the miners grew and grew in intensity and eventually the miners set Horymír's property on fire. In retaliation, Horymír and his followers burned down the miners' village. Horymír was caught, punished, and swiftly sentenced to death. He was given one last wish and he used that to ask to take one last ride around the castle grounds (Vyšehrad) on his beloved horse - Šemík. His wish was granted. Horymír got on his white horse and whispered something in the horse's ear. Šemík immediately galloped across to the Castle ramparts, jumped over them in one large leap and slid down the cliff. When the bemused on-lookers finally got to the ramparts, they saw Horymír and Šemík in the distance on the other side of the Vltava River, already galloping back towards Neumětely.

Unfortunately, the miraculous jump over the ramparts had exhausted Šemík who, speaking to Horymír in a human voice, asked that a suitable tomb be prepared for him. Horymír did as the horse wished. While the tomb has long since disappeared, legend says that Šemík is sleeping in the Vyšehrad rock, ready to come out when his help is needed again - echoing the Arthur in the cave legend in England.

The Naming of Smíchov

When Vojen, also one of the six Dukes, came to power, he was too young to rule so a man named Rohovic was appointed to govern for him. Rohovic proved to be a stern and cruel ruler and eventually, the people decided they would prefer the young Vojen, rather than Rohovic, to rule. Rohovic resisted, but was finally defeated and sent into exile, where he turned to a life of crime, preying on people in the Lučko region. In order to try to stop this, Vojen sent a messenger to order Rohovic back to Prague. Rohovic's response was to send him his messenger's head back on a stake. After a long siege of Rohovic's stronghold, Vojen's men finally captured him and brought him to Vyšehrad where Vojen sentenced Rohovic to death on the riverbank opposite the castle. While in the boat crossing the river, Rohovic, continued to curse and threaten Vojen. As he was finally executed, evil spirits were heard to laugh out loud and the place was named Šmichov, meaning *laughter*, as a result.

The Czech culture is full of such magical and mysterious tales preserved for posterity by telling and retelling over hundreds of years. The Czech culture is replete with these strange fairy tales, legends, and myths. Perhaps, it is partly down to the Czech's love of beer drank by the bucketful every night in pubs and bars all across the country. As the best beer in the world is drank each evening, it creates a wonderful environment for people to swap stories and tell tales. One can readily imagine that a combination of the alcohol, the pagan origins of the Slavs (Catholicism is the dominant religion, but it is only a minority profess a religion. Communism took its toll of organized religion and probably even helped create this myth and legend environment) and wonderful countryside, helps sustain these tales.

Ghost Stories from The Czech Republic

As might be expected, the country is absolutely full of ghost stories and I have covered many of them below in order to give a sample of the types of tales and stories prevalent here. The Prague ghost stories in particular are often rather whimsical and one wonders how many are real stories and how many were manufactured to help entertain tourists on the many ghost tours that are available there?

Prague Ghost Stories

As might well be expected, the majestic capital city of Prague is full of ghosts and stories of hauntings. In fact, Prague is probably one of the most haunted cities in all of Europe, with its rich history of magic, murder, and the bizarre. During the reign of Emperor Rudolf II, it became the center for astrology, magic, alchemy, and the esoteric, attracting people like John Dee (see later). Consequently, the architecture of Prague includes all kinds of esoteric and magical symbols, which can reveal many secrets to those who know how to read them.

Here are a number of Prague ghost stories.

The Ghosts of 27 noblemen

In a rebellion against the Habsburg monarchy in 1618, several Bohemian nobles conspired together and ended up throwing two governors and a secretary to their deaths from a window of the Prague Castle. They had been forced to convert to Catholicism or face banishment from their homeland by the monarchy and they rebelled.

Figure 3: The Charles Bridge, Prague

After a crushing military defeat at Bilá Hora by the Imperial forces, some forty-seven Czech nobles were put on trial and more than half of them sentenced to death. That sentence was carried out in 1621 and a total of 27 noblemen were executed at Prague´s Old Town Square in one morning. You can still see 27 white crosses marking their deaths in the square by the old astronomical clock.

The executions began early at 5 a.m. in the morning. Prague's executioner, one Jan Mydlář, performed the executions with four keenly sharpened and carefully prepared swords. Twenty-four of the nobles were beheaded and another three were hanged. A contemporary drawing of the ghastly scene shows two bodies dangling from a beam protruding from a window in the Old Town Hall in Prague, while another body hangs from a gallows.

Mydlář, a Protestant himself, sympathized with the nobles, but he was forced to do his ghastly job. Wearing the traditional red executioner's hood, he stood sharpening his swords and dealt with his bloody work that day as swiftly as he could. The nobles knelt on the scaffold facing away from him and one by one they met their bloody end but cleanly. He did his work so skillfully that an English spectator later wrote that the heads appeared to have been 'blown from the shoulders of the victims'. With a single stroke, one man after another's head flew into the Old Town Square, where soldiers kept the crowd at a distance.

When the executions finally ended at 9 a.m., Mydlář took twelve of the heads, put them in iron baskets, and suspended them from the towers at both ends of Prague's Charles Bridge; six on each tower. One of the nobles widow asked to be allowed to claim her husband's head and bury it with the rest of his body; she received permission but a year later. The other eleven heads remained rotting on the bridge for approximately twenty-years. When the heads – now only weathered skulls – were finally taken down and they were buried under the floor of the Protestant Týn Church on Old Town Square, near the execution site.

The noblemen now reputedly haunt the Charles Bridge, calling out to passersby late at night. They are also said to rise from their graves in the Church of the Holy Savior once a year to view the Astrological Clock on the Old Town Hall.

The Prague Golem

One of the city's most popular legends is the story of the Golem of Prague. Visitors to the City will find evidence of the Golem everywhere in café and pub names and in small statuettes sold on almost every street. The legend involves the Rabbi Judah Loew who created the golem to protect the Jewish quarter of the city and its citizens. The golem was made of clay and then animated by the Rabbi. During this time, many of Prague's Jews were being attacked and lived in fear of persecution.

Rabbi Loew created the golem using Cabala magic and the clay from the banks of the Vltava River that runs through the city. The golem proved to be highly effective scaring the city's inhabitants to the point that the city's politicians promised to end the persecution of Jews, if the Rabbi would stop his terrifying golem. He did so and the remains of the golem are said to be hidden in a secret room above the temple of a synagogue in the City. It is also said that the secrets of remaking it are still located somewhere there.

Laura

The ghost of a young actress named Laura haunts Malá Strana in Prague. Laura was a married woman and a popular actress that fell in love with a Count. When Laura´s angry and violent husband discovered the affair, he sent the Count a gift of an ornate wooden box containing Laura´s severed head. Her ghost is still searching for her head and now it haunts the Dominican Monastery in Prague.

Knight Templar

A Knight Templar is believed to ride along Liliova Street at midnight carrying his own severed head under one arm. His spirit will only rest if someone has the courage and the strength to seize his horse´s bridle, take his sword and run it through his heart.

Dalibor The Violin Player

The Prague Castle complex includes the Daliborka Tower that was originally used as a prison until the end of the 18th century. It was designed to hold only nobles as prisoners initially, but later became a prison for commoners as well. The tower is named after its first prisoner, Dalibor from the village of Kozojedy.

Dalibor was a young and brave knight who was sentenced to death and kept in the dungeon of the tower. While imprisoned in the Tower, he learned how to play the violin. Over time, the sounds of his violin playing became familiar and welcome to the citizens of Prague who would visit the Tower to listen to him play. He became so popular with the people that his execution date was never announced. The people only knew that Dalibor had been executed when the sound of his playing was no longer heard. These days, visitors to the Castle sometimes hear ghostly violin sounds emanating from the tower.

The Repentant Priest

One evening, as a priest walked down Celetná Street, one of the local prostitutes decided to play a joke by flashing herself at him. The priest was outraged and in a momentary fit of anger, he hit her with his crucifix, killing her instantly. When he realized what he had done and that she was dead, he also dropped dead in the street. They now are said to both haunt the location.

One-Armed Robber

Visitors to St. James church in Prague can see a strange and gruesome object hanging from the ceiling if they look up on entering the church. It is a 500-year old severed human arm. The story of how it got there is also very strange. A thief, who was hoping to rob the church, was supposed to have been grabbed and held in a vice-like grip by a statue of the Virgin Mary before he could steal anything. The stone statue gripped his arm so tightly that the only way to release him was to cut off his arm, which was then hung in the Church to dissuade other would be thieves. The one armed thief now haunts the doorway of the church where he likes to show people his severed arm socket.

The Headless Skeleton

Another Prague legend says that every Friday at midnight, a black coach drawn by black horses travels down Janskÿ Vršek Street. The occupant of the coach is a headless skeleton that is on fire and covered in flames. After a short drive along the street, the coach and its occupant simply vanish, sinking into the ground. The origins of the flaming skeleton driving a carriage are unknown.

St. John of Nepomuk

St. John of Nepomuk, one of the national saints of the Czech Republic, once took a confession from the Queen of Bohemia. Her husband, King Wenceslas IV, asked what it was that she had said to the priest and when St. John refused to tell the King what he had heard, the King had St. John tortured and then hung in chains off Charles Bridge until he died.

It is apparently true that the King tortured and killed St. John, but the reason was more likely a disagreement over a new abbot, not for keeping the Queen's confession a secret. However, many still believe that by touching the statue of St. John of Nepomuk on Charles Bridge, you can keep any secret safe and the bronze, brightly polished by thousands of hands, shines strongly as a result.

Berka

Another quaint story of unhappy romance involves a soldier named Jachym Berka. Returning from war, he was told many unsavory rumors regarding his fiancé and other men and as a result, he broke up with her. She then threw herself in to the River and drowned herself and when her father learned of this, he too committed suicide throwing himself from a tower. Of course, when Berka discovered what has happened and how he had been mislead by gossip, he hung himself. These days, the unhappy ghost of Berka is said to wander through Prague in full body armor seeking a virgin who will walk with him. In the Old Town district of Prague there is a monument to this unhappy Iron Man; probably the only statue of a ghost in existence.

The French Soldier

Then there is the ghost of a French soldier killed laying siege to Prague in 1741. His ghost used to patrol the walls of Vyšehrad, attacking passersby. Apparently, sick of this ghosts' attacks, in 1892 the Austro-Hungarian Army honored this fallen Frenchman to appease his ego. Apparently, this worked for now the ghosts is said to walk the walls with a smile on his face.

The Turk

A Turkish man also haunts Týnský dvůr. He became engaged to a pretty young Czech woman and then returned to his homeland to ask his parents' permission to marry her. As the Turk was gone for a quite a long time, his fiancée, hearing nothing of him, began to believe that he had died, or that he had simply forgotten about her. When the Turk finally returned to Prague he found that the young woman had just been married and was celebrating with her family. She disappeared that night and the decapitated body was found later. That Turk offers passersby a glimpse into the box that he holds and haunts the courtyard. Visitors should be warned that the box contains the young woman´s freshly severed head.

The Fires of Petřin Hill

Petřin Hill is a beautiful hill down from the Prague Castle complex that is topped with a small tower that offers superb views of the city of Prague, and rose gardens. It also features a funicular that can be ridden to the top of the hill and back down again for a small fee. However, Petřin Hill has a sinister history and was once the site of an altar used by early pagans to make human sacrifices, mainly young virgins, to their Gods. A Christian Prince - Prince Boleslav – took exception to this pagan cult and had them dealt with, destroyed the pagan site and built a church there instead. However, this was not the end of the matter as the pagan Gods are credited with starting small fires on the hill from time to time. The fires last around 20 minutes and if you are present when one starts, you are supposed to be able to see the victims of the pagan sacrifices within the flames.

The Miller's Daughter

A rather horrible ghost that is reputed to knock old people over, chase after young men, and throw herself on young pretty ladies biting and scratching at them in anger also haunts the Lichenštein Palace. She behaves this way as a result of selling her soul to the devil to gain entry to a ball at the palace. She was a simple miller's daughter but she had dreams of marrying a wealthy nobleman and after trying every way she could think of to obtain an invitation to the ball, she made an arrangement with the devil and got her way. However, the story says that she was ignored at the ball and ended up screaming and carrying on in such a way that was carried from the ball by a group of men. After this shameful event, she led a normal life until she passed away when she was claimed by the devil and put into his service haunting the castle.

The Fish Eater

A large park called Stromovka in Prague boasts a Fish Eater, a sort of vampire that feasts on the blood of rotting fish but should you be passing through the park on a moonlit night, may just be tempted to try a drop of human blood too. The Fish Eater was once an aide to General Windischgratz who held various posts in the Austrian army but notably was head of the army in Prague. He was a strange man who hailed from an aristocratic family and was related to Count Dracula. He would bathe on moonlit nights in the fishponds of the park imagining himself as the head officer of the fish in the pond who he saw as his soldiers. Unfortunately, he met a bloody end at the hands of a man named Vondra who beat him to death with a stick. Vondra threw his battered body into one of the ponds where it lay undiscovered and rotting for a long time. Of course, he could have become a regular vampire but his long sojourn in the mud and water of the fishponds was said to have weakened him to the point where he instead became a Fish Eater.

Talking of ponds, the Czechs also have a water spirit called Karbourek. Karbourek is somewhat affectionate and kindhearted and lives in the Devil's stream. Occasionally, he is said to beg passers by for a mug of beer and those who reward him so are supposed to be given a pike or an eel in return.

One of the most famous characters in Czech fairy tales is also a water sprite called "vodník" or "hastrman". You can see him anywhere close to water and he embodies the spirit of water. He is usually depicted as green man riding on a catfish. He has green hair, bulging eyes and water is dripping from his coattails. He is usually described as an evil spirit that likes to harm people and who catches inexperienced swimmers in order to gain their soul.

He is very resourceful when it comes to catching souls and will use ribbons and small mirrors to lure girls into the water, for example. He can also change himself into all kinds of animals such a horse. However, if somebody tries to ride him while he is a horse grazing by the shore of a pond, he jumps into the water with the person on his back and drowns them. He stores his gathered souls in a jar at the bottom of the pond.

Then there are the *rusalki*, female ghosts, mermaids, or water-demons that haunt lonely lakes or rivers. *Rusalki* are believed to be the souls of unbaptized children, suicides, or unwed mothers who died in childbirth, living in a state of purgatory.

Vincenc, The Skeleton

Another ghost you might meet in Prague is a skeleton however; you need to be drunk first. A young man called Vincenc used to work at the medical facility that used to be in the Kaolinum. He was tall and elegant and one of the anatomy Professors joked with him that one day, he'd like him in his skeleton collection. The young man struck a deal for his skeleton with the Professor after he was dead. Unfortunately and tragically, he got very drunk with his newfound fortune and got killed in a bar fight. Now, his skeleton ghost hangs around the area asking other drunks for their spare change so that he can buy his skeleton back.

The Mad Barber

The ghost of a mad barber can sometimes be seen on Karlova Street. He is a mild-mannered ghost that is seeking his freedom from an eternity of wandering the streets of Prague's Old Town. He lived during the reign of Rudolph II and was a successful barber but his profession didn't provide enough money to keep him happy so he tried his luck with alchemy.

He practiced the ancient art in his home and magically started to produce gold. In the end however, greed destroyed him and he spent all of the family's money and was left with nothing. He was forced to sell his house; all three of his daughters became prostitutes and his wife, jumped to her death. The barber went mad and started to slash passersby with his razor until he was beaten to death. It is said that in order to free the Mad Barber, a brave young man must agree to let the mad barber shave him.

The Haunted Hotel

In searching for other ghost stories during my research for this book, I came across a rather remarkable review of a Prague hotel in Trip advisor. The Residence Green Lobster is a luxury four-star hotel in Prague 1. It got the following 5-star review on TripAdvisor.com in 2011.

My wife and I stayed at the wonderful Green lobster hotel and we had the first suite on the first floor. The suite was amazing and more than comfortable, we have to say by far the best hotel we have stayed at in our trips to Prague.

However, we did believe there was a little bit of spiritual activity in the suite to keep us both entertained.

Both my wife and I struggle to believe in anything like that but if it's in your face, you can't argue can you?

The first thing was a light stroking of my face on the first night that woke me up with a jolt I can tell you.

The second night I experienced nothing, but my wife had a sentence whispered to her in Czech, that she could not say back to me as neither of us speaks Czech.

The third night I heard some say to me "help" and we both awoke to see the small cupboard in our room open, however this was strange as it was locked shut!

However, on our last night it was the most active, we both awoke at 4:30am to the sound of someone walking around and moving things about in the room directly below us.

I went to check but it stopped instantly, half an hour later, we awoke again to a sound of dripping water?

I checked the taps in the room downstairs but all was fine and the sink was dry, I am a Plummer By trade so I know when something's not right.

We went back to bed and slept without another incident, until the morning came and my wife could not find her phone.

We turned the place upside down, and found nothing, until my wife went to put her shoes on and found it under   her   shoe?
All in all, we were not bothered by what went on, if anything it added a little more character to the suite that was already amazing in our eyes. We will stay here again as we loved it, and the staff made it a joy to stay at as well.

Thank you Green Lobster hotel for giving us a wonderful stay and experience.

Just to note I wonder if anyone else has had an experience like this at this hotel?

Plainly, the visitors found the ghosts good value. Knowing Prague, I have to believe that many hotels in the old town are also haunted.

Other Locations

The white Lady

The white lady is a very famous ghost in the Czech Republic. She is reputed to have been Perchta of Rožmberk (c. 1429-1476) who was the remarkably beautiful daughter of an important Czech nobleman - Oldřich II of Rožmberk. She spent an idyllic childhood at the family castle in the beautiful town of Česky Krumlov. Later in life however, as was common for nobles in those days, she was forced to marry a certain Jan von Lichtenstein, who had a reputation for being something of a mean old brute of a man.

The marriage was, to say the least, quite unhappy for not only was Jan horrible to her, but his sister and the sister of his previous wife were even worse, mistreating Perchta daily. In the end, the tormented and extremely unhappy Perchta wrote to her brother begging him to take her away. He did so and Perchta finally returned home to her family, but it is said that she never smiled again in her entire life. She was later reunited with her horrible husband just one more time on his deathbed when he begged her to forgive him. Perchta refused and Jan is said to have placed a curse on her in revenge.

Perchta died in 1476 and now her ghost is said to walk the estate owned by her family as an apparition known as the 'white lady'. Apparently, if you ever see her, it is extremely important to note her demeanor for if she is smiling then good news will follow but.... if she looks serious and wears or carries black gloves, then the news will be bad!

There are many stories about the white lady. She is always dressed in a white drew and veil. She was apparently very taken with the young Petr Vok, one of her ancestors, when he was a baby often appearing peering over his cot. The nurse grew suspicious of the ghost and one night took the child away causing the white lady to abruptly vanish through a wall. Years later, when he was an adult, he was told of this occurrence and found a magnificent hidden treasure behind the wall that the white lady had passed through.

The white lady was also often seen on the ramparts of the castle. In one sighting, the castle was being worked on and there were scaffolds supporting parts of the walls. A worker saw the white lady one day behind the ramparts and assumed that it was someone standing on the scaffold. However, when he reached the spot, the lady had vanished and to his amazement, there was no scaffold at that part of the castle.

The Tragedy of Fairytale

Pohádka means fairytale in Czech but it is also the name of a reputedly haunted and cursed location. It all began May 1828 when in a nearby village called Strážov, a fire broke out. One house caught fire and a storm blew hot embers across the roofs of neighboring houses. In the end, 78 houses including the town hall were destroyed. The villagers wanted to know why such a horrible event would take place in such an idyllic place and soon they had an answer. Near Pohádka, by edge of the forest, was a small hut occupied by a strange old woman. There was talk of her being a witch. This poor old woman was determined to be the culprit and to be the cause of the fire. She was chased from her home, stoned, and killed. However, not before she had cursed the place.

The curse apparently took effect and people in the area have suffered as a result. One inhabitant went mad after finding her husband hung in the house and another committed suicide after his wife and children disappeared in the forest never to be seen again. The last occupant was one Ivan Roubal. He was recently convicted for murdering five of his neighbors. Two of his victims' remains were never found and it is believed that Ivan fed the bodies to his pigs.

A Czech Vampire and the Czech Undead

In Žďár nad Sázavou, a Czech vampire once roamed. Alois Ulrich was an unkindly man and administrator of the local castle estate. He treated his fellow humans with the same contempt that he had for his animals. In his early 60's, he suddenly contracted a very strange disease and succumbed. No one was particularly sad to see him pass away.

He was buried in the lower churchyard. However, Alois continued to terrorize his neighbors, even in death, as he was seen by many villagers both in the cemetery and standing on a local bridge. There was even a murder attributed to the dead Alois. The increasingly concerned and scared inhabitants of the town called on a local landowner to investigate. They decided first to make sure that Alois was actually dead and buried; so, they exhumed him. When the coffin was opened, they found that the body showed absolutely no signs of decay and when they called him by name, Alois opened his eyes and slowly sat up. The local Priest tried to talk to him but Alois only snarled back. The solution was to sever his head with a spade and to fill his mouth with poppy seeds as an anti-vampire measure. He was then cemented into his grave. That solved the problem.

Belief in the undead in the Czech Republic and surrounding countries is strong and given the proximity of Dracula, there may well be good reason. However, it seems that belief in the undead goes back in the Slavic culture much further than to Dracula. The best evidence of this was found in Čelakovice in Central Bohemia during the construction of some houses there. Archaeologists found the skeletons of fourteen people dating back to the late 10th or 11th Century that seemed to have been tampered with after death. They had been buried with their hands and feet tied up, mouths clogged with dirt and they were all positioned face down. The idea being that in this position and tied up, they could not climb back out of the grave. If this sort of burial didn't solve the problem, then the solution was to dig the grave and sever the heads with a spade. Four of the skeletons at Čelakovicka were found in this state and one even had a wooden stake driven through the left side of its chest!

An early recounting of vampirism in the Czech Republic dates to around this time. In about 1250, in Liebava near Olomouc, a vampire would leave his grave in the local cemetery at night and walk into the town attacking women and children who were asleep before returning to his tomb in the early hours. He was readily identified as a man who had recently died by those that had seen him. The vampire was taken so seriously as to call upon the services of a Hungarian vampire hunter. The Hungarian spent several nights watching the grave from the bell tower and once he saw the man emerge from the grave, he snuck down and stole the man's shroud. When the vampire returned, he was enraged to find it gone and began to climb the bell tower in anger to reach the Hungarian. However, the Hungarian lay in wait armed with a sharp shovel and severed the vampire's head in one expert stroke.

Yet another account from 1337 is of a number of vampires in a church in Opatowicze. The area was exorcised and sprinkled with holy water and crucifixes. That apparently solved the issue.

The famous Montague Summers, a clergyman and author who wrote about supernatural creatures including vampires, concluded that the belief in vampires was strongest in the Czech Republic and that Bohemia was a center of vampire activity. He recounts a really horrific tale of vampirism from the village of Blov in Bohemia. He tells of a herdsman that h begun attacking and murdering fellow villagers as a vampire after his death. The village exhumed his body and drove a stake through his heart, making sure that he was pinned to the ground. Unfortunately, the same night the dead herdsman rose again and continued his murderous activities, even gloating that the villagers had done nothing but *"given a fine stick to drive the dogs away"*. The killing was apparently only stopped when his body was finally cremated.

Velhartice Cemetery

The cemetery at Velhartice is supposedly a very, very scary place. Firstly, on the side wall of the small chapel in the cemetery are dark spots that seem to resemble faces. Even if painted or freshly plastered these spots soon reappear again. This is said to be as a result of an original small wooden chapel being burned down by robbers with some locals trapped inside it. There is also a story made famous in a well-known Czech poem about a local girl whose fiancé returns from the war. Being very happy to see him, she at first isn't suspicious about his request to marry in the middle of the night. Off they go to get married at midnight and the girl becomes increasingly suspicious of his behavior especially when they end up at the cemetery. That is when she realizes that her fiancé is in fact dead. She hides in the mortuary and survives until morning when she makes her escape.

Amerika Quarry

One of the most spectacularly beautiful places in the country is the Amerika quarry, which is said to resemble the Grand Canyon in a miniature way. A member of the German army called Hans Hagen is said to haunt the quarry. He was apparently trying to escape the Red Army and wanted to be caught by the Americans (who did liberate part of the Czech Republic). He hid himself in the limestone caves of the quarry to evade capture by the Soviets. There he lived in darkness, stealing food and supplies as he could from the miners. At some point, Hagen went insane under these conditions and when finally caught and trapped by the miners, he killed himself. Shortly afterwards, Hagen was said to be terrorizing homeless people in the area and was reportedly last seen in 1965 stealing canned food. He ran away screaming and laughing. The story became even stranger with the 1969 discovery of two bodies with their heads torn off in the quarry. One head was eventually found but the other still remains missing to this day.

Ostrov Castle

Ostrov is a small town near Karlovy Vary. A small Chateau in the town was the subject of recent fantastical news headlines when a CCTV camera seemed to capture a ghost in the building. The Nazi SS used the Chateau during the war as a concentration camp for people opposed to the Nazi regime. The place has a sinister atmosphere and a reputation for items going missing. After many items simply vanished, the staff looked at the CCTV camera footage and discovered that it had caught the image of a dark shadow crossing and re-crossing the room the camera was in late at night when the building was empty. In the video, a shadow crosses in front of the camera several times.

For the scared staff, this discovery was no surprise, as they had felt uncomfortable in the building, now operating as a museum, many times before. The ghost is believed to be that of former owner of the Castle, Franz Joseph Heinrich Graf Schlik zu Bassano und Weisskirchen. According to family legend he always carried a silver box with him full of coins and important documents and, even in death, he is protecting his valuables.

Castle Divci Hrad

There are several legends about Divci Hrad, which is close to Mikulov in Moravia. One such legend talks about a secret treasure hidden somewhere deep beneath the castle while other legends are about beautiful maidens. One involves a beautiful and rich Princess who was invited to stay by the local Lord. Tempted by her wealth, he murdered her and then threw himself from the cliffs in remorse. These days, the Princess wanders the forests around the Castle as a white maiden.

Sirotci Hradek

This Castle is close to Hrad Divci in the Mikulov area and according to legend, there was a Templar knight who lived there. He refused to go off to a battle because his wife was about to give birth to his first child and son. The Templar knights sent another knight to find out where he was and the wife asked him to became a godfather to their child and to name him. He named him Sirotek (Orphan) and killed his father to make him a real orphan. The widow died of a broken heart, and Sirotek was taken away. Sirotek returned after many years and found an old servant who had survived the massacre and learned what had happened to his parents. He became crazy and these days his ghost can be seen riding on a horse around the castle.

Creepy Places

Anyone who has ever visited the Czech Republic and managed to actually leave the delights of Prague for other locations, will know that it is a rather beautiful country that still retains vast forests, wild gorges and valleys and small, somewhat isolated villages. A goodly portion of the country especially north and east of Prague, was once covered in pale-colored sandstone that has now weathered out into magnificent standing columns and ridges of rock. One can find narrow crevices, caves and enchanted places in these sandstone forests and one can certainly imagine how the local's imaginations might create and weave stories to explain their landscape. In other areas, such as around the city of Brno, the landscape is dominated by massive limestone karsts that are also full of caves and amazing forested scenery. Such a landscape bestows a feeling on the person surrounded by it of magic and nature spirits. Now,

Figure 4: A passage way between stone skaly

add to this mix literally tens, if not hundreds, of amazing castles with long and often barbaric histories, and you have the recipe for amazing legends, tales, and myths. These often include ghosts, wraiths, and strange humanoids like elves and imps. They also include mysterious cracks that are said to lead to the gates of hell.

Branišovský Forest

Branišovský forest is a creepy haunted forest close to the city of České Budějovice and it has so many urban legends, myths and ghosts stories associated with it, that it's very hard to say what may be true or false and where to begin in recounting these lurid stories.

One such story is about a number of soldiers who were killed there. Back in communist times, the forest was the site of a local armory. Two soldiers were on guard duty and about to be replaced by two others when something horrific emerged from the woods. Three soldiers were killed on the spot by gunfire and a fourth died later in hospital. In fact, part of the mystery is that stories vary about what actually happened. In one version, one or two of the soldiers transformed into something horrific, in another version, it was jealousy that caused the shootings and yet another says two of the soldiers suffered from some sort of stress response and started shooting the others. Whatever happened there is no record of the incident in the official military archives. Yet, that has only deepened the mystery as investigators claim that the event really happened, was covered up by the authorities and that secret documents exist covering this strange event.

Another strange story involves a tree, the hanging tree, in the forest. After several people were found hanging from the tree having committed suicide, the tree gained an evil reputation. The people found hanging there had no known reason to commit suicide and one such event involved the wife of a newly married couple. A local woman who was collecting firewood decided to cut the branch off of the tree and burned it, thinking this would stop the rash of hangings. Her hand withered and was crippled after removing the branch. In the end, a group of villagers took matters into their own hands, cut down the entire tree, and burned it on the spot. Now, people wandering the woods who come across the site of the hanging tree report strange voices in their heads telling them to kill themselves.

The forest is also the home of a ghostly man in black. He was first sighted in the 1990's and is said to be a tall man with a pale and indistinct face, dressed in black clothes and cloak whom moves very quickly, floating just above the surface of the forest. Some have reported hearing strange music just before sighting him and others have described a sudden drop in temperature prior to his appearance.

The forest also has a reputation for creepy noises and other strange phenomena. People hear footsteps crunching the dried leaves on the ground. Some say they have been chased by an invisible entity that may in fact have been the man in black. Others have reported being watched by a pair of slanted red eyes after dark. There is also reputedly a white lady ghost in the forest.

Perhaps the most intriguing phenomenon is that involving lost time and leaps in time. In 1960, a local resident set out on a journey that usually took an hour on foot. As he arrived at his village, he noted that no lights were on at all in any of the small homes – unusual for 9pm at night. On arriving at his own home, he discovered that it was actually 3am and he had lost many hours in time. In another incident, a woman in a party of walkers ran into the bushes and simply disappeared for 45 minutes. When she returned out of the very same bushes, she told her friends she had entered a sort of greenish mist and then into a strange place with the lights of a city in the distance. The man in black had then appeared and pushed her by the forehead back out into the forest. While for her the whole incident was a matter of seconds, she was gone almost an hour.

A Gate To Hell? - Houska Castle

Are there portals to other dimensions, other existences, or planes? Well, if there are, one scary example might well be Houska Castle situated about

50km north of the Czech capital city, Prague, also known locally as *The Gate To Hell*.

Figure 5: Hrad Houska

Over 1000-years ago, much of the Czech countryside would have been dense forest. In the Houska area, those forests would have been dark, gloomy, damp, and eerie as the area is famous for its sandstone formations known as 'Skaly'. The sandstone in the area erodes out into block-like formations that jut ominously in many locations, creating an eerie but beautiful landscape. Millennia ago, this landscape would have been like an alien world for the sparse populace in which the imagination would and could run riot! There were few settlements and fewer people who still clung to many pagan beliefs about woodland spirits, demons and ghosts. Not surprisingly, the area developed an evil reputation. Demons and half-human monsters were said to roam the deeply incised, tree-covered valleys, seeking human and animal victims and warm blood.

Figure 6: Typical Skaly rock formations

The discovery of a deep crack or fissure in the sandstone certainly wouldn't have helped matters much in terms of the areas' terrifying reputation. Efforts to fill the fissure with stones and boulders failed. In fact, they had no impact whatsoever. The fissure seemed endless; a crack of doom in the Earth's surface from which that knows what monsters, elementals, and spirits emerged? Rumors suggested that this fissure without end was a gateway to hell and that demons and spirits used it as a route to Satan's fiery regime for wicked hell-bound human souls and the innocent victims of demonic activity in the area. Local farms mysteriously lost animals and passers by avoided it in the darkness.

Something had to be done and at some point in the 900's it seems as if a Chapel was built over the crack in the Earth in an attempt to close it and lock out the demons. In fact, no one is really sure when the Castles' structure really was built, as mysteriously, the records have all disappeared. This fact is even more dramatic given that the Czech Republic is littered with fairytale-like Castles each with a thoroughly documented and proud history. The first mentioned structure on the site however was a small wooden fort in the 9th Century though it is believed that a structure might have existed on the site since the 6th Century. Part of Houska's mystery is that it is the exception to the rule in not having a documented history. In fact, it doesn't even appear on some maps; as if it were meant to be a secret that was kept secret.

The story of Houska becomes even stranger however, for as the structure was being built, the Landlord agreed that which ever condemned man would be lowered on a rope into the crack in the rock to describe what he saw there, would be freed. A volunteer was lowered only a few feet into the hole in the Earth before he started screaming hysterically. He was immediately retrieved and found to have suddenly developed snow-white hair, aged at least 30-years and had become quite mad. He died the following day without divulging what horrors he had seen in the gate to hell. One can imagine that work resumed on the Castle with even more urgency than before.

The Castle or structure that was built there was also very strange. It had defensive structures facing inside the castle as opposed to outside, to keep out intruders. Rather, it seemed designed to keep something in. Although it had several floors, there were no stairs connecting the floors and additionally, it had fake windows in the upper stories. It was a very strange Castle indeed. Added to that was its' location, which was far from anywhere and not on any pathway or road. It did not have a source of water and it was for all intents and purposes a castle that was built where no castle would normally ever be constructed.

Figure 7: The Left Handed Centaur

The fissure or endless hole apparently now lies beneath the floors of a small chapel. Painted on the walls of the inside of the chapel are some rather strange designs that include

Figure 8: St. Michael and the Dragon

the only known example of a female left-handed centaur shooting a man with an arrow. On another wall, is the image of St. Michael plunging his lance into the mouth of a fearsome dragon. Other images include St. Christopher, an angel weighing human souls and the Christ. Having stood in the Chapel myself, I can tell you that there is an energy there that after only a short while becomes unbearable. I had a headache for several hours after leaving. Interestingly, these murals add mystery to the Castle as being left-

59

handed in medieval times was thought to be a sign of evil (the left-hand path) and St. Michael was the Archangel tasked with fighting hell's hoards. Despite all of this, strange sounds, moans and screams are said to be heard coming from below the Chapel and people have claimed to see demonic entities there, including a strange creature that looks like a cross between a human, frog and giant bulldog.

Over time, various nobles owned the Castle and its structure was changed and altered so that today, it is more of a small chateau than a castle. During the Second World War, the Nazi SS again occupied it; this is puzzling as why would a Castle in the middle of nowhere or of no strategic value be used by the SS? Many believe that the SS was running some kind of occult experiments there, perhaps with the energy portal, or another theory is that it was an experiment in creating the master race – a place where German SS troops would seed blonde haired Aryan women in the hope of creating a superior race of humans. No one knows for sure and the retreating Nazis destroyed all the records of what actually took place there.

Another strange tale regarding Houska that adds to its mystery and intrigue is the letter written by a famous Czech writer who spent a night there in the 1800s. In his letter to a friend, he recounts hellish dreams in which he visits 2006 Prague where a girl shows him moving pictures in a 'small casket' (iPad?) and he drifts by huge sandstone cliffs with square holes emitting yellowish light (very much like a description of modern apartments blocks that now litter Prague).

The Castle has also hosted other wicked and strange historical characters as if it were a beacon of darkness with some significance known to practitioners of the dark arts. One of these was the Swedish rogue commander of a mercenary army that chose Houska as its headquarters. Oronto was thought to be a black magician and alchemist who performed certain experiments at the castle. He and his soldiers terrified the local population who eventually summed up enough courage to shoot him. Even today, the courtyard of the Castle often contains tens of dead birds that have to be cleared.

Houska's reputation for evil and strangeness is also

Figure 9: The Chapel at Houska

recounted in the various tales of visitors who even now have experienced strange feelings at the castle and have experienced bad luck. The third floor is said to host the ghost of a beautiful young woman and paranormal activity has manifested on that floor with a glass that levitated in front of a group of people. Another visitor to the Castle saw two darkened figures that were muttering something about killing some young girls.

The Castle now hosts conferences and meetings on a variety of supernatural topics and is thought by some experts to be an energy portal that was recognized by the Nazi SS, Oronto, and others through history and used accordingly. However, if Houska, is an energy portal what is a portal to? Other dimensions? Who knows? However, this mysterious place with its foreboding atmosphere and strange Chapel decorations remains a mystery that continues to attract visitors and the curious to its walls.

Zvikov Castle

Zvikov Castle is actually quite a beautiful castle that stands at the junction of the Vltava and Otava rivers about 15 km north of the town of Písek, in South Bohemia. The area was inhabited even in prehistoric times, and the Celts built a fort there in the 1st century AD. The current castle was constructed in the 13th century. The oldest part of the castle is a tower called Hlízová that seems to pre-date the main construction and may even date back to the 1st Century. However, the tower is also to be avoided as anyone sleeping there is supposed to die within the year.

The tower is decorated with strange and unknown symbols and is thought to haunted by the Zvíkovský Rarášek, a creature similar to an imp. The Zvíkovský Rarášek is described as a small creature with a red hat and fiery eyes that scare most people, but may also bring good luck. The creature inspired Czech playwright Ladislav Stroupežnický, to write a famous play of the same name. The imp or trickster plagued the workers who constructed this original tower driving them away and gaining an everlasting reputation in the process.

Weird things happen at the Castle including strange photographs, technical problems with electrical equipment, electromagnetic anomalies, strange animal behavior, ghost sightings, and so on. Since the Castle is so picturesque, it has been the location for several Czech films (The Czech independent film industry has always been strong and they make a lot of fairy tale movies utilizing such Castles). Sometimes, plans to film in certain parts of the Castle had to be changed due to camera problems, batteries dying very quickly, fogged film, and even a strange shadow crossing a hallway and disappearing into the wall in one shoot. Another strange occurrence during filming was the constant unexplained extinguishing of fires and firelights being used by the filmmakers.

Finally, fire hounds or spectral dogs with red eyes are sometimes seen around the Castle and these are thought to protect and guard a secret tunnel underneath the castle. The tunnel is said to lead to a treasure but the treasure is not gold and silver but a spiritual treasure.

Kutná Hora

In a town named Kutna Hora, there is a very famous ossuary that is said to contain the bones of between 40,000 and 70,000 people. The site, which is beneath the cemetery of the Church of All Saints just outside of Kutna Hora, is a very creepy visit. Delightful human skeletal chandeliers hanging from the ceiling accentuate four huge bell-shaped mounds of bones in

each corner of the Chapel. There is even a coat of arms - all made from human skeletal remains, on

Figure 10: Skeletal Chandelier

the wall.

The story behind how this came to be is equally fascinating. Back in 1278, a monk returned from the Holy Land with soil from Golgotha. This was spread in the cemetery, making it a much-wanted final destination for many people in the region. The results of a 14th Century Black Death outbreak and 15th Century wars in the region also ensure that there were many thousands buried there during that period as well. The ossuary was created when rebuilding work meant digging up many of the bodies in the 1400's and this practice continued to make room for new tenants in the cemetery for several

hundred years. The macabre decorations in the place were the brainchild of a woodcarver given responsibility for

Figure 11: Bone Coat of Arms

the place in 1870.

The place has a very strange atmosphere. It is probably just the imagination - but who knows? With some 50,000 remains, there surely there must be one or two spirits haunting the place?

Brno Ossuary

In 2001, a startling discovery was made in Brno during a survey of catacombs under the center of the city. Although disturbed by underground water and mud, the remains of 50,000 people were found stuffed into a small room. The room was floor to ceiling with the skeletal remains of the City's former inhabitants. After restoration work, the Brno Ossuary was opened to the public in 2012 and is the second largest Ossuary in Europe after the Paris catacombs. So how did they get there?

In the 16th and 17th Century, due to cholera, the Plague, war, and so on, people tended to die in large numbers periodically. They were buried in the churchyard near the Church of St. James inside the city walls however, to cater for such numbers in a limited space, they were dug up again several years later and the remains stored in the crypt of the church. Their graves were then occupied, or perhaps we should say 'rented', by the newly dead who would be moved 12-years or so later. Eventually, due to health reasons, the churchyard was closed and all the bodies moved to the crypt as well. During this time, the crypt had to be expanded and made larger to hold all of the remains of what is estimated to be 50,000 souls.

You can visit the Brno Ossuary and see the remains for yourself if you dare. I can tell you this, it is creepy, and the thought of constantly digging up bodies and placing them in the crypt is pretty freaky too.

The Capuchin Crypt

Here in Brno is one of the creepiest places I have

ever visited. It is known as the Capuchin Crypt. On the outside, it is nothing but yet another small but ornate church but inside... It is Brno's

Figure 12: Capuchin Crypt, Brno

strange and creepy mummy show....

The Capuchin monks who used the church for many years were an order who vowed poverty. As a part of this austerity program, they used just a single coffin over and over again, laying the body of their dead colleague on the ground, rosary in hand, in the crypt. Due to the nature of the soil and the air currents down there, the bodies became mummified. Each body was laid on the floor with its head on a pile of bricks that served as a pillow. The practice was later stopped by the introduction of new hygiene laws in the 19th Century. The result however, is that there remain 24 partly mummified monk bodies laid out carefully in the crypt.

It's not just monks however, that lie in the creepy crypt but also benefactors of the order including Baron Trenck and Baron Franz Josef Kotulińskich with his wife Eleanor. These and other notables lie in glass-topped coffins adding to the gloom and eeriness of the place.

A small entrance fee is all that it takes to visit the site where you will also be greeted with the sobering painted statement on the crypt itself - *As you are now, we once were; as we are now, you shall be.*

Faust House, Prague

One of the most mysterious places in Prague is Mladotovský palace also known as Faust House. The house has had many owners who dealt in alchemy and magic, conducting chemical experiments in the hope of making gold or the elixir of life. In the 14th century, the keen naturalist and avid alchemist, Prince Vaclav of Opava, owned the house. During the reign of Rudolf II, the astrologer Jakub Krucinek lived there with his two sons. The younger son killed his older brother for the treasure alleged to have been hidden in the house. The building was later bought by the court alchemist of Emperor Rudolf II - Edward Kelley (see below). He set up a laboratory in the house and carried out various chemical experiments. Kelley claimed that he could transform lead into gold but he too failed.

Later, in the 18th Century, Ferdinand Mladota of Solopysky, who also had an interest in alchemy and physics, owned the house. He scared his neighbors with loud explosions and other experiments along with automatically opening doors and other mechanical contraptions. He managed to set the house on fire once conducting experiments, which led to the local people blaming the Devil and his worship at the house, for the fire. The houses bad reputation continued with a former chaplain of the church who was passionate collector of skulls and other creepy items and even slept in a coffin.

It is also believed that more recently, a student living in the House tried unsuccessfully to patch the expansive holes in the ceiling. The student found a book of secrets, magic, read some of the spells, and was magically taken through the holes by the devil, much like Dr. Faust and that resulted in the nickname of the house.

Veveří Castle and The Templar's Treasure

For several centuries, treasure hunters have looked for the Templar's treasure at Veveří castle, near Brno. There have long been tales about the Templars of France who brought their valuables there right after the dissolution of the order in 1307. Recent research at Veveří has actually confirmed the existence of an underground space under the church near the castle. To deepen the mystery, there is a cipher of the name Molay, the last Grand Master of the Templar Order, above the entrance to the church.

Vyšehrad Cemetery

Last year, I visited Vyšehrad. According to Wikipedia, Vyšehrad *(Czech for "upper castle") is a historical fort located in the city of Prague, Czech Republic. It was built, probably in the 10th century, on a hill over the Vltava River. Situated within the castle is the Basilica of St Peter and St Paul, as well as the Vyšehrad Cemetery, containing the remains of many famous people from Czech history, among them Antonín Dvořák, Bedřich Smetana, Karel Čapek, and Alphonse Mucha. It also contains Prague's oldest surviving building, the Rotunda of St Martin from the 11th century. Local legend holds that Vyšehrad was the location of the first settlement that later became Prague, though thus far this claim remains unsubstantiated.*

It is the Castle founded by Libuše and the site of the episode with Horymír and his horse. I found it a truly beautiful place, but the Cemetery really freaked me out.

Although the Cemetery is probably the place that many famous Czech's aspire to be laid to rest, it took me several days to shake off the total gloom and despair that I felt after visiting it. The whole time I was there, I kept seeing shadows in the shadows, and, when I turned around, I could swear I was being watched. The presence was truly evil and left me with a feeling of being lost in a nightmare. I never actually saw a ghost, so to speak, but I am convinced something unpleasant resides there and it's not a place I would want to be in after dark. Maybe, it's the art nouveau tombstones, the stark black marble tombs, or perhaps it really is just haunted, but I shudder recalling being there.

The Ghost Of Baron Trenck

Baron Trenck's mummified remains are part of the horror show that is the Capuchin Crypt in Brno. He also spent some time incarcerated in Brno Castle and it is there that his ghost is said to walk through the halls close to where his cell used to be. Our Baron though, also has his ghostly fans. Rumor has it that every year during the Feast of all Saints, a ghostly woman can be seen kneeling and praying at the side of his mummified body in the crypt.

The Child with The Bell

In Josefka Street in Brno, there is a pub in which the ghost of a baby is sometimes seen. The story behind this sighting is that the baby's mother worked in the pub and upon discovering, she was pregnant, she decided to kill the child at birth. Sure enough, the Mother killed the newborn and buried its remains in the basement of the pub. Now, the child's silhouette is seen holding a small bell.

Other Ghosts of Brno

Brno is the Czech Republic's second city and unsurprisingly, it too has a collection of lurid ghost stories. Apparently, lights will come on by themselves on the first floor of the New Town Hall building. A man can be seen walking sadly in the courtyard of a house in Jánská Street, holding the sword that he was murdered with. Ghostly monks are seen wandering in the area of what would have been the corridors of the long gone Jesuit Monastery in the city center and the Dominican convent of St Anne is also reputed to be haunted by the ghost of a woman who went insane.

There are many other stories such as that of a house on Křídlovická Street where every night, the occupants hear rumblings on the upper floors of the building said to be the ghost of Prince Ypsilantiho who spent many years under house arrest there. A piano is often heard playing at Česká street despite there being no piano in the vicinity. My favorite however, is about Kohoutovice forest in Brno-Jundrov, where a shouting woman is often seen on the edge of the forest. A drop in temperature often accompanies her appearance and a white cloudy figure has been seen between the trees.

The Brno Labyrinth

Under the Vegetable Market in Brno are a series of tunnels and cellars collectively known as the Brno Labyrinth. You can even take a short-guided tour of these connected cellars. What you will see on the tour are a lot of old cellars that were constructed below what was a very busy market square in the center of Brno. They were used to store produce and to keep that produce fresh for as long as possible.

However, that is not all that was stored down there for a certain Countess Amalia, a beautiful and clever lady, would take her lovers' bodies into the tunnels to hide them there after she had murdered them. There are supposed to have been 13 men knifed to death by this lady who now wanders the tunnels, walking with a cane and laughing hoarsely, sometimes swinging her knife and searching with her cane to be sure that the remains of her lovers stay safely hidden.

Nedamov v Dubé Poltergeist

A home that was being repaired in the village sparked some media coverage literally when many objects in the house simply burst into flames. Over a six-day period, some 45 fires burned including non-combustible items. The home had burned down without any attributable cause and was being rebuilt. The workers there also were threatened by events like a saw blade being thrown so hard at a wall that it stuck in the wall and other objects flying around.

Boletice Cemetery

Boletice cemetery is the site of an interesting tale regarding two cantankerous old souls who argued even after death. Dead and buried in the cemetery, the pair was heard to continue cursing and arguing so loudly that nearby homes had trouble sleeping. Eventually, the Priest sought advice on how to handle the phenomenon from Rome and was told to place the crosses on both graves back to back to each other. After this was done, peace finally reigned in the cemetery.

You can't take it with you... can you?

There is a wonderful tale of an old miserly farmer who lived near Kájov. Before he died, he asked to be buried with a head pillow. Sure enough, his family did as he wished, but then no sign could be found of his wealth, which was reputed to be considerable. After a lot of searching, they dug the old man up. The old man lay stiff in his coffin grasping his pillow tightly. Of course, the pillow was full of money and despite how hard they tried, they could not retrieve the pillow or the money and had to bury him with his money. I guess that was one old guy who did try to take it with him?

Bohnický hřbitov
The cemetery in Bohnice, Prague, is old and in disrepair. It contains some 4,000 souls and was open and used between 1903 and 1963. It resides in the gardens of an old and disused psychiatric hospital and unsurprisingly is thought of as Prague's scariest cemetery. Being disused and abandoned, the cemetery became the place for Satanists to conduct rituals during the 1980's and not surprisingly, it is supposed to be haunted. Strange sounds and sights are often seen at night and the cemetery is a regular haunt of ghost tours. The graves, largely of insane asylum inmates along with at least one murderer and a number of first world war soldiers, are covered in ivy and overgrowth and the place has been vandalized many times making it a very creepy after dark visit.

Other Strange Czech Tales

The Devil's Bible

A few years ago, I had the opportunity to see this strange document first hand, as it was on display outside of Brno. In fact, what I saw was a copy of the original. Nonetheless, the effect was chilling. The Devil's Bible or *Codex Gigas* is 36inches tall by 20 inches wide and about 9 inches thick. It contains a set of Christian texts including the Bible. It is bound in leather with metal trim and weighs over 165 pounds. It is known for the amazing color illustration in its pages of the Devil and that is how it gained its name.

Historians believe the text was created in the Benedictine monastery of Podlažice in the Czech Republic in the early 13th century. Now, as if the scale of the Bible wasn't enough, the Bible's creation legend is even more bizarre. A monk in the middle Ages, who, after breaking his monastic vows, was sentenced to the horribly cruel death of being walled up alive, is said to have written it. Desperate to avoid his fate, the monk promised to write – in just a single night – a book that both glorified his church and also contained all human knowledge. His plan was accepted but by midnight, he was nowhere near completing the book. He decided he needed help but instead of praying to God, he prayed to Lucifer offering his soul in return for the finished book. The Devil responded to the monk's prayer accepting the offer. Within seconds, the huge book was completed while the monk added the portrait of his mentor and savior in gratitude. Although, some say Lucifer himself painted the picture.

Experts agree that one person wrote the entire book and estimate it would take more than 5-years to complete – at least without supernatural help anyway.

The Black Ambulance

In the 1980's, an urban legend grew very quickly in Prague and elsewhere regarding a black ambulance that abducted children and sold them for their organs. How the legend got started is anyone's guess but soon children were reporting being followed by strange black vans and cars and there was such panic that the Czech State Television had to run a special program to debunk it. Apparently, this was just one variation on an urban legend regarding black cars and vans that took root across the old Soviet block at the time.

Roadside Shrines

One thing you will note if you drive anywhere in

the Czech Republic are small roadside shrines. These are often fashioned as small houses or chapels and that is exactly what they really are. They are essentially Christianized versions of pagan spirit houses, which were built for the souls of the

Figure 13: A Typical Czech Roadside Shrine

dead. The local pagans burned their dead to free the soul from the body so that the spirit could leave for the after life. The old Czech pagans set up these small shelters at junctions to help these spirits find their way.

Čert

The Devil pays a focal role in Czech myth and legend. He threatens the kids every year before Christmas on St. Nicholas' day in a tradition that has Čert, an Angel and St. Nicholas (Mikuláš) asking the children if they have been good. Good children get gifts and bad children end up in the Devil's sack and are dragged off the hell.

Čert is another throwback to pagan times when the pagans believed in demons that could ruin crops, create bad weather and kill. "Čert" (the devil) originates with an old Slavic word - "czart," the name of a malevolent pagan demon that haunted bogs and springs.

Čert is not necessarily an evil being in Czech myths and fairytales. Quite often, he is engaged trying to get humans to sell their souls for something in return – much like in the story of the Devil's Bible (money, power, completion of task). Usually, those tricked get nothing or something useless and end up being dragged off to hell anyway. Sometimes, *Čert* is himself tricked by the hero who gets his soul back.

Čert is usually portrayed as a hairy man with horns, tail and perhaps hooves, but can appear as other forms too. Whether Čert is the Devil or not depends. Quite often, hell is full of Čerts and the Devil is their boss. Whatever the case may be, Čert is a big part of Czech myth, legend, and culture.

John Dee & Edward Kelly – Alchemists at The Court of Rudolf

Dr. John Dee looked every bit like a wizard. By the end of his life, he had a flowing white beard and wore a skullcap over his thinning hair, so that he probably would not have looked out of place at Hogwarts. Edward Kelly, his sidekick, was an altogether different sort of character. He was a necromancer, a confidence trickster, and a commoner who used his ability to talk his way into money and power. One died an old man, living out his final years in relative obscurity back in England, while the other died a violent death falling from a high window while making an escape attempt from Prague jail.

During his wanderings across Europe, Dee met many famed people, including Cornelius Agrippa, another very famous magician. Agrippa and Dee investigated natural magic and telepathy together. Queen Mary of England invited Dee, whose fame as an astrologer had spread widely, to cast a horoscope for her forthcoming marriage. Mary's sister, Elizabeth, was imprisoned at that time, and Dee also drew her horoscope. The two became friends. Once again, Dee was in hot water, though, as he was accused of trying to murder Queen Mary using black magic. He was eventually acquitted, and when Elizabeth was crowned, she invited him back to her court.

In the years that followed, Dee, and his wife started to have strange dreams about contacting spirits. As a result of this and his general interest in the esoteric, he tried used a magic mirror and other scrying instruments to attempt contact with the spirits. However, Dee was forced to conclude that he wasn't that good at scrying, and so he hired others to do it for him while he took notes of the communication. This was how he met Edward Kelley.

Edward Kelley was a rogue who had already had his ears clipped as punishment for some crime that he committed. He was a conman and trickster, but he too had an interest in magic and the occult as he is reputed to have engaged in necromancy and to have raised the freshly dead body of a young woman, re-animated it using black magic, and then questioned it about the whereabouts of a small fortune. Dee was probably aware of his new colleague's reputation, and so he made Kelley promise not to work with evil spirits.

After meeting a Polish nobleman at Elizabeth's court, the pair was invited to Poland where the nobleman funded their continued experimentation with spirit communication as well as the far more potentially profitable venture of alchemy. Rumors abounded of Dee and Kelley turning various base metals into gold using a mysterious red powder they had developed; but in fact, these may have just been rumors as, after two years, the Polish nobleman went broke supporting the pair.

From there, they went to Prague and the court of Rudolf, who at the time had gathered a host of famous alchemists and magicians. However, they were accused of sorcery again by the Pope and had to leave Prague, eventually settling in Trebon, in what is now the Czech Republic, yet again supported by a rich nobleman. It is here that a truly bizarre event took place. Kelley claimed that the spirit Madimi had instructed Dee and Kelley to share their wives with each other. Dee was married to a much younger and, almost certainly, attractive woman; and one has to believe that Kelley, the conman, saw his opportunity. Initially, Dee and his wife refused, and the pair went their separate ways. However, Dee must have agreed in the end, as a document was signed by all four swearing to carry out all the commands of the angels.

This event must have been deeply traumatic, and one wonders if Dee didn't begin to suspect Kelley of manipulation as, not unsurprisingly, their relationship soured. Dee and his wife returned home to England where Elizabeth I gave him the wardenship of Christ's College, Manchester, and he eventually died peacefully at age eighty-one. As for Kelley? He was killed making an escape bid from a Prague prison where it seems his luck had finally run out.

Frantisek Bardon – The Czech Master Magician

Frantisek, or Franz Bardon as he is more commonly known, was a Czech magician who was unfortunate enough to be persecuted by both the Nazis and by the

Communists for his amazing magical and healing powers. Strangely enough, when I look out of my office window here in Brno, I see Brno Castle sitting stark upon the skyline. It is less than a half-kilometer walk from where I live, and that is where Franz Bardon died in chains in a communist prison back in 1958.

Franz Bardon was born in 1909 in Opava in the former Czechoslovakia. What we actually know about Bardon comes from the four key magical works that he wrote or had a hand in writing, and from the recollections of a few former students and his surviving family. One of the books is a semi-autobiographical account of his life called *Frabato the Magician*, and it is here that we perhaps learn most about Bardon. Like his character Frabato, Bardon made his living performing as a stage magician in Germany. He was, we are told, a stage magician, but one with a difference—he used real magic, hypnosis, and he did not resort to sleight of hand or trickery.

His magic show involved amazing people with clairvoyant readings of objects, including recognizing what the hidden object was and then providing a history of the object as well as its owners.

The stories surrounding Bardon are actually very strange, and many even border on the bizarre. For example, Bardon, the only boy amongst twelve daughters in his family, changed in character and ability almost overnight at age fourteen, amazing his family and teachers. His father, a spiritual man himself, had prayed for guidance and for a spiritual teacher all of his life. The advanced soul that was Franz Bardon answered the father's prayers by taking over the body of his then fourteen-year-old son. Throughout his life, Franz Bardon suffered from poor health, and he attributed this to taking on the karma of the original Franz Bardon who had agreed to vacate the body he took in order to allow the master to have one!

Another strange but verified as true story involves a student of Bardon. Although instructed to burn his correspondence with Bardon as he had been instructed, he failed to do so. The Nazis found this correspondence, and the pair of them ended up being thrown into a Nazi concentration camp after Hitler had tried to recruit Bardon as a magician to aid his war efforts. From being offered power and money as a key part of Hitler's regime, Bardon was tortured, operated on without anesthetics, and chained to heavy metal balls. He even had a job of collecting severed heads from the scaffold in the camp apparently. One day, as they were being beaten and forced to work, the student uttered a cabalistic magical phrase (essentially a magic spell *a la* Harry Potter) that caused the Nazi guards to become frozen and immobile. When the spell was reversed, the student was shot and Bardon tortured. After serving several years in the concentration camp, Bardon too was sentenced to death, but the Allies liberated the camp on the very day that he was to be executed. After the war and his escape, Bardon helped people clairvoyantly locate their missing relatives.

Figure 14: The Tomb of Franz Bardon in Opava

Whatever the truth regarding Bardon and his origins, without having any real access to the occult literature of the time, he became a true spiritual guru and a master magician with students of his own. He wrote three classic books on magic and its practice that you can still purchase today, and he has something of a global following.

Frabato the Magician was most likely actually written by Bardon's secretary, who based it on Bardon's own notes after his death in Brno Castle at the hands of the Communists. If the book is based on the truth—and the publisher who knew Bardon's secretary claims that she was honest and truthful to a fault—then Bardon was not only an amazing physical magician and healer, but also an exalted soul who was and still is working with the higher spiritual powers governing this Earth to direct its spiritual evolution.

One of my favorite accounts in the book is of Frabato (**Fra**nz **Ba**rdon **T**roppau **O**pava) walking with one of his students. Frabato (or Bardon) makes it rain to show his mastery of the elements, and the rain starts to fall in buckets from thunderstorm clouds that suddenly appear from nowhere at Bardon's command. The student, who is not dressed for the weather, gets soaked to the skin as they walk and discuss magic. Meanwhile, it doesn't rain on Bardon at all, and he remains miraculously dry, comfortable, and calm during the entire incident.

In that book, Bardon, who is performing magic shows in Germany, comes to the attention of a very evil order of magicians indeed; one that even Hitler was reputed to belong to. In failing to recruit him to aid the war effort as a powerful magician, they set out to destroy him with magic. The satanic lodge is described as having a maximum of 99 members and a demon to make 100. In turn, this lodge was one of 99 other lodges. Each year, the lodge recruited a new member and then drew lots to see whom the new member would replace. The unfortunate soul who is to be replaced is then ritually killed by magical methods, and his personal demon granted to the new member. Each member of this satanic and evil magic lodge is allocated a demon that sees to their every whim and need, whether sex, money, power, or all three.

Bardon uses magical means to defend himself, defeats the master of the lodge who commits suicide and for eternity must serve the demon that had served him. He was summoned back to Czechoslovakia, to an astral meeting of the masters, to be told that he may disclose previously jealously guarded spiritual knowledge to aid in the spiritual evolution of humanity. Although he finds this instruction to go against everything he was taught during his magical training, he concurs and writes the three books of magical instruction that one can still purchase today.

Eventually, Bardon, now making a living healing people, had gained a powerful reputation for miraculous cures using herbs and tinctures that he prepared himself at home. People came from all over Europe to be healed, and his reputation included healing cancer and other terminal diseases. He was eventually arrested by the Communists on the pretext of using illegal alcohol in preparing the medicines and in illegally dispensing those medicines, and he was imprisoned. All of his magical notes and instruments disappeared somewhere deep within the communist machine and, as a result, we are left with very little except the sources mentioned above.

Bardon died as mysteriously as he lived. He had his wife deliver some bacon to the prison, which upon eating, set off a pancreatic condition. Though in agony, the guards assumed he was faking the pain, and he died. Every day as I walk down my street here in Brno, I look up at the stark castle on the hill, and I reflect on the magician and the master that incarnated as Bardon and then expired from that incarnation just a stone's throw from where I live.

Býčí Skála

To the north and west of Brno is the limestone karst of Moravia. It is full of natural caves many of which you can visit. One actually served as a nuclear bunker for Soviet forces during the cold war. However, it is Bull Rock (Býčí Skála) that has captured many imaginations in the past. This cave was found to contain all sorts of skeletal remains – mainly young women with their heads and limbs severed. Many archeologists believe that this was a shrine were human sacrifice was conducted in Paleolithic times. Today, many say that they have heard the screams and shouts of these victims, both human and animal, as they were sacrificed to the old

Gods in what must have been a gory and brutal ritual.

The Church of Nine Ghosts

In the town of Luková in the north of the Czech Republic, a medieval church that had fallen into disrepair, has become a creepy tourist attraction after artist Jakub Hardrava was finished with the place. The ceiling of St. George's church had collapsed back in 1968 and it had lain abandoned ever since. Then, in the summer of 2014, the artist placed inside the church a number of plaster ghost statues. The statues represent the ghosts of the Sudeten Germans (repatriated to Germany after WW2) who used to use the church. These days, this creepy work of art is attracting tourists and the curious to this little town. To see just how creepy it is, take a look at this you tube video of the place.

Summary

The truth is that ever Castle, town and village in this small country, has its own myths, specters, and strange creatures lurking in the dark and gloomy forests. It truly is fit to qualify as the most haunted country in the world.

Given that the country has its own thriving movie business that has churned out endless fairy tales over the years, perhaps it isn't surprising that the Czech's enjoy their stories. Every school holiday, the TV channels show the same old favorite fairy tales so that each generation of Czech's have a common grounding in the strange myths and legends of the Slavic peoples. The bookstores (books are very popular here) are filled with fairy tale and hauntings books too. The dark pagan past is an undercurrent that is not too deeply hidden in Czech culture evidenced by some of the holidays and Christianized activities that take place on those holidays.

I love supernatural stories so if you have had any encounter with the strange forces that underlie our reality, please do share them with me at myhauntedlifetoo.com.

Many thanks.

Don't forget to drop by and submit your encounters.....

About G. Michael Vasey

 Growing up can be extremely tough for any kid, but imagine growing up around poltergeist activity and ghosts? G. Michael Vasey had exactly that kind of childhood, experiencing ghosts, poltergeists, and other strange and scary supernatural phenomena. In fact, he seemed to attract it, developing an interest in the occult and supernatural at an early age and he has been fascinated ever since.

His "My Haunted Life" trilogy has been highly successful—reaching number one on bestseller lists on both sides of the Atlantic. Now he is presenting the stories of others. The second book in the "Your Haunted Life" series is currently available on Amazon. It's a must-read for anyone with an interest in the strange happenings of the paranormal world. Then there's "The Pink Bus And Other Strange Stories From LaLa Land," a book that lifts the veil on one of the biggest mysteries in human history—the process of death, and what happens to our souls when we die.

He has appeared on numerous radio shows such as

- Everyday Connection,
- Jim Harold's paranormal podcasts,
- True Ghost Stories Online and
- X Radio with Rob McConnell

sharing strange and scary stories and his expertise in all matters supernatural. He has also been featured in Chat - Its Fate magazine and been interviewed by Ghost Village and Novel Ideas amongst   others.

Whether you've heard one of G. Michael Vasey's radio appearances, or read one of his books over the shoulders of an avid reader on the bus, or whether you've simply got an interest in the paranormal and stumbled upon this page... You are going to pulled into the paranormal world of G. Michael Vasey, and you will be hooked.

You can discover much more about the supernatural at www.gmichaelvasey.com, read true scary stories at www.myhauntedlifetoo.com, or tune in to his tweets at @gmvasey.

Other G. Michael Vasey Books

- **The Black Eyed Kids - Your Haunted Lives 3** (Kindle and audio book)
- **Your Haunted Lives - Revisited** (*Kindle and audio book*)
- **Your Haunted Lives** (Kindle, audio book and paperback)
- **The Pink Bus** (*Kindle and audio book*)
- **Ghosts In The Machines** (*Kindle and audio book*)
- **How To Create Your Own Reality** (*Paperback, Kindle and audio book*)
- **God's Pretenders - Incredible Tales of Magic and Alchemy** (*Kindle and audio book*)
- **My Haunted Life - Extreme Edition** (*Paperback, Kindle, audio book*)
- **My Haunted Life 3** (*Kindle, eBook and audio book*)
- **My Haunted Life Too** (*Audio book, Kindle and ebook*)
- **My Haunted Life** (*Kindle, ebook and audiobook*)
- **The Last Observer** (*Paperback, ebook, audio book and Kindle*)
- **The Mystical Hexagram** (*Paperback and Kindle*)
- **Inner Journeys - Explorations of the Soul** (*Paperback and Kindle*)

Poetry Collections

- **Death On The Beach** *(Kindle)*
- **The Art of Science** *(Paperback and Kindle)*
- **Best Laid Plans and Other Strange Tails** *(Paperback and Kindle)*
- **Moon Whispers** *(Paperback and Kindle)*
- **Astral Messages** *(Paperback and Kindle)*
- **Poems for the Little Room** *(Paperback and Kindle)*
- **Weird Tales** *(Paperback and Kindle)*

All of G. Michael's Vasey's books can be obtained on any Amazon site and some can be found on other book sites such as Barnes & Noble, Apple and more.... He offers signed and dedicated paperbacks from his website at http://www.garymvasey.com

Made in the USA
San Bernardino, CA
15 September 2017